D1491599

The Fool or Joker, the one unnumbered card in the Tarot pack, symbolizes folly, hesitation and their resultant ills.

sacred symbols

The Tarot

Thames and Hudson

THE TAROT

Its origins shrouded in mystery, the Tarot pack constitutes a body of potent and far-reaching symbolism. The most solid evidence, however, indicates that the Tarot originated in the fifteenth century as a pack of playing cards, when Bonifacio Bembo painted an unnumbered deck for the Visconti family of Milan. Games with the cards – sometimes using packs of varying extent – then spread through northern Italy and into the rest of Europe, but the first direct description of them did not appear until 1659 in France. The connection of the Tarot with the occult and divination looks back to a relatively short tradition begun by Antoine Court de Gébelin (1719-94), a Protestant pastor and Freemason from Geneva. His beliefs – essentially that the Tarot represented aspects of the Egyptian mysteries – were taken up by occultists on both sides of the Atlantic towards the end of the nineteenth century, notoriously by the Order of the Golden Dawn, which counted W.B. Yeats and Aleister Crowley among its members.

Whatever its origins, the symbolism of the Tarot does lend a richness to the use of the pack for divination. Perhaps, as Jung suggested, man repeats archetypal patterns from his unconscious, even if the cards have no direct descent from ancient wisdoms and mysteries. These patterns embody the real fascination of the Tarot: the counterpointing of good and evil, of the male and female principles, and the interaction of the four elements: Air, Water, Fire and Earth.

Modern Tarot packs are based on the Italian deck known as 'Venetian' or 'Piedmontese', consisting of twenty-one numbered Trump cards and one unnumbered card (the Fool or Joker), and four suits of ten 'Pip' cards and four Court cards. Many packs are notable for their graphic brilliance and ingenuity; the illustrations in this book have therefore been drawn from a wide range of designs through the ages – a beautiful introduction to a subject of infinite depth and complexity.

THE MAJOR ARCANA

The strange, esoteric symbolism of the Tarot Trump cards exercises a compelling attraction through its vivid yet ambiguous imagery. Here, portrayed through the archetypes of religious and secular experience, are the great issues of life; these are the cards which go to the underlying principles of existence. Taken as a whole, the sequence, from one to twenty-one, is often compared to a journey from childhood to death, followed by resurrection. In other words, a rite of passage from innocent beginnings to final illumination.

I
The Magician

This figure neatly exemplifies the transition of the Tarot through the centuries from being simply a playing deck to a means of divination. Traditionally, he was shown selling various objects from a table or stall, while bearing a wand indicative of his skill and magical powers. His other hand points to the objects before him to symbolize his ability to control practical affairs. In later versions of the card, a wand, cups, sword and coins can be seen set before him – the four key elements of practical life, the four suits of the Tarot and a multi-layered opportunity for the fortune-teller.

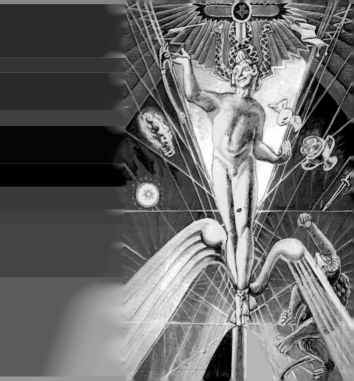

The High Priestess

In traditional Tarot packs this card was referred to as the Papess, or Female Pope; she is associated with the dream world, the realms of the unconscious and with intuitive knowledge. She is often seen seated between pillars, known as Boaz and Jakim, or Alpha and Omega, a reference to the pillars of the Temple in Jerusalem; one is coloured black, symbol of the feminine principles of mystery and intuition, while its white pair expresses masculine rationalism.

KEY ASSOCIATIONS
True, intuitive wisdom and knowledge;
the feminine side of the male personality.

REVERSE ASPECTS
Superficiality; lack of personal harmony;
suppression of the feminine or intuitive side
of the personality.

3
The Empress

Associated with the more practical, motherly aspects of the female principle, this figure may be represented as a dignified though kindly, queen-like presence, sometimes surrounded by symbols of fertility, a reference to child-bearing, marriage and home-making. The Empress is practical, kind and generous in her attitude to others.

KEY ASSOCIATIONS
Steadfastness in action; promotion of well-being and security.

REVERSE ASPECTS
Lack of action and concentration; possible domestic problems, even difficulties in child-bearing.

4
The Emperor

Responsibility and firmness are present in every aspect of this omnipotent figure. The sense of power is expressed in his posture: he faces sideways, thus distancing himself from the viewer. His control of the physical world is indicated in his crossed legs which form the figure of '4' – the four elements.

KEY ASSOCIATIONS
Ability to shoulder
responsibility;
forcefulness in
development and
execution.

REVERSE ASPECTS
Opposition to authority;
immaturity and
indecision.

5
The Hierophant
or Pope

A symbol of religious authority in the traditional Tarot pack, this figure is now more likely to be associated with the idea of informed professional advice or counselling. The hierophant – priest of the sacred mysteries of Greece – may be accompanied by two other figures in the foreground of the card, who are the seekers after knowledge and benediction. Sometimes these are represented simply by hands reaching up to touch the vestments of the holy man.

THE POPE

KEY ASSOCIATIONS
*Religious guidance and
authority; constructive
counsel.*

REVERSE ASPECTS
*Dubious advice; misleading
and inappropriate comment.*

KEY ASSOCIATIONS
Making difficult decisions, not necessarily about love; considering important commitments.

REVERSE ASPECTS
Postponing choices; being indecisive or making bad decisions.

6
The Lovers

This card has been subject to a number of representations and interpretations through the ages. The traditional form, of which there were a number of variants, showed a man choosing between two women, while a corpulent Cupid directed his arrow at the suitor's heart. Later versions of the card show Adam and Eve in the Garden of Eden, although these tend to obscure the card's main associations with choice and making the right decision.

7
The Chariot

The chariot in question is drawn by two horses without reins (in some versions they may be replaced by sphinxes). The charioteer, crowned and in armour, is thus seen to be directing the horses by sheer will-power, hence the association of the card with the human ego and ambition. Some cards show one black and one white horse – the female and male principles – indicating that the various conflicting aspects of personality have been brought under control by strength of character.

KEY ASSOCIATIONS
Ability to overcome adverse situations;
ambition and decisiveness in achieving
one's ends.

REVERSE ASPECTS
Loss of control; chaos in one's personal life
and disregard for others.

8
Justice

One of three of the four Cardinal Virtues to be represented in the Tarot pack – the others are Fortitude and Temperance – Justice has been subject to shifting representations. In some packs, for instance, she appeared as card 11, while card 11, Strength, was switched to 8, to coincide with the order of the Zodiac and their respective associations with Libra and Leo. Like the other virtues, Justice is a woman, sitting in a judgement posture and holding the traditional sword and scales.

KEY ASSOCIATIONS
Fair and reasonable judgement;
triumph over bigotry and prejudice.

REVERSE ASPECTS
Unfair or delayed judgement;
inequality and bias.

9
The Hermit

The traditional representation of this figure is as an old man wearing a long habit and carrying a lantern; this is sometimes replaced by an hourglass, suggesting a connection with time and patience. Since the hermit is one who has isolated himself from other human beings, he may be seen to symbolize independence and introspection, a need for soul-searching. If this card appears during a reading it will probably indicate a need for reflective, individual decision-making.

KEY ASSOCIATIONS
*Need for prudence;
need to reach into
one's inner resources.*

REVERSE ASPECTS
*Isolation from others;
a negative resistance
to help.*

The Wheel of Fortune

The central motif of this card is the wheel itself to which a number of animals cling precariously. Above the wheel is a presiding figure, which may sometimes take the form of the goddess Fortuna or that of a sphinx.

The dominant theme of this card is clearly the role which random events play in our lives in the form, hopefully, of good fortune and unexpected luck. A reversed card, though, can indicate the exact opposite – chance misfortune which may strike in spite of all our efforts to achieve a favourable set of circumstances.

KEY ASSOCIATIONS
Unexpected good fortune;
success without striving.

REVERSE ASPECTS
Failure in spite of all efforts;
unexpected bad luck.

24

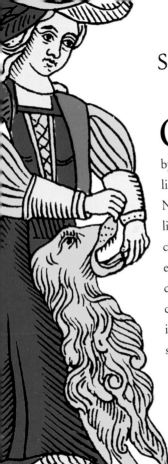

II
Strength

One of the Virtue cards in the Tarot pack, Strength may be personified by a woman holding open the jaws of a lion, or by Hercules in combat with the Nemean lion. In a positive sense, the lion can represent inner strength and courage, as long as the powerful emotions in play have been properly channelled and controlled. A reversed card here has very negative implications, indicating an inability to exercise self-control.

KEY ASSOCIATIONS
Strength and power under control; the Virtue of Fortitude.

REVERSE ASPECTS
Feelings of inadequacy and powerlessness; power wrongly used.

KEY ASSOCIATIONS
Devotion to worthwhile ends;
sacrifice in pursuit
of a greater good.

REVERSE ASPECTS
Lack of commitment; apathy
in pursuit of goals.

12
The Hanged Man

This is one of the most mysterious cards in the pack and one which has defied most attempts at a satisfactory explanation of its significance. The central figure hangs by one leg from a cross-piece, but is usually portrayed with a contented expression on his face. Some versions show coins falling from his pockets, as though to indicate that he is giving up worldly and material wealth, thus associating the card with the concept of sacrifice.

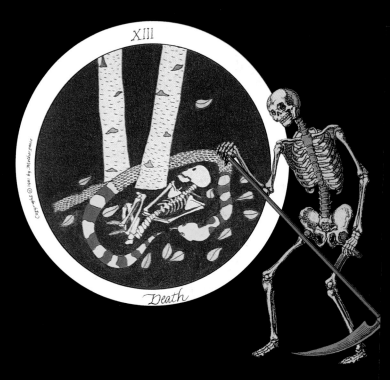

Death

In most versions this card displays a personification of death in the form of a skeleton wielding a scythe, surrounded by the severed limbs of recent victims. But in spite of its gruesome aspect, Death is rarely an indication of actual death, but rather of the change from one phase of life to another. This can even be a happy occurrence, such as the beginning of a new relationship, although there is a strong implication that the change must be accepted with a positive attitude.

KEY ASSOCIATIONS
Change and alterations;
the beginning of a new life.

REVERSE ASPECTS
Unpleasant, painful change;
slow and possibly agonizing
periods of transition.

14
Temperance

As all Virtue cards, Temperance is shown as a woman. In most cases she is a winged figure seen pouring some liquid from one flask to another; the prominence of the wings on the figure's back has led some commentators to speculate that her origins are angelic, although it is more likely that she is derived from winged female figures of classical antiquity. The passage of the liquid from one container to another indicates the need to find the right blend in all things, to mix various elements until the correct balance is found.

KEY ASSOCIATIONS
*Balance, especially in
matters of personality;
maturity in handling
difficult circumstances.*

REVERSE ASPECTS
*Conflicting interests;
fickleness in making
decisions.*

The Devil

The most common image on this card is the depiction of the central figure of the Devil, sometimes winged and sometimes in the form of a goat, below which are two other demonic figures apparently leashed around the neck. Another variation shows the Devil as a horned god, perhaps derived from the Celtic stag god, which had associations with fertility ritual. Like Death, the meaning of this card is not direct; rather than symbolizing all things truly demonic, its main connotation is of inconvenience, of the unpleasant details which are an ineluctable part of life.

THE DEVIL.

KEY ASSOCIATIONS

Disturbance and ruin; sudden, violent loss.

REVERSE ASPECTS

Less severe forms of the above.

The Lightning-struck Tower

Although this card seems to indicate total disaster at first sight, as with most of the more alarming cards in the Tarot pack, there is a somewhat brighter side. The immediate image, though, is disturbing enough: a tower capped by a crown struck by a

thunderbolt, causing the occupants to be hurled through the window to their deaths. The crown is shown to be dislodged by the bolt, which may indicate a blow to the personal ego. But while the card does undoubtedly signify something very disturbing and possibly violent, there may sometimes be the implication that something useful can be learned from the experience. Reversed, the card may indicate a less severe form of experience than in its upright position.

17
The Star

The dominant figure of the card is a naked woman pouring water from two flagons on to the ground. Some commentators have identified her as the Babylonian goddess Ishtar who sought the waters of life to revivify her dead lover. In the sky behind the figure is a very large star surrounded by seven smaller ones, possibly the Pleiades. The theme of restoration to health and life is dominant here, especially after a period of tribulation and stress.

KEY ASSOCIATIONS
Renewal and fresh hope;
promise of fulfilment.

REVERSE ASPECTS
Diminished life; some
obstacles to happiness,
but this can still be
achieved.

18
The Moon

This is a very negative card: an old woman's face fills the moon at the head of the card – another aspect of the feminine principle, but now implying age and loneliness. A dog and wolf howl at the moon while, from the pool in the foreground of the image, a sinister-looking crayfish crawls, like a vision from the murkier depths of the spirit. There is a strong sense of lack of direction and confusion, of being caught in a web of personal error.

KEY ASSOCIATIONS
*Personal depression;
confusion arising from
an inability to see things
clearly.*

REVERSE ASPECTS
*Exaggerated forms of the
above; despair and a desperate
need for help.*

19
The Sun

One of the most optimistic images in the Tarot pack, the sun signifies high ideals of achievement and feelings of balance and happiness. The traditional representation of the sun itself is with a human face which beams down benevolently on twin children apparently standing in a walled garden. Sometimes a child may be shown mounted on a horse, an animal traditionally associated with Jupiter and therefore a potent solar symbol.

KEY ASSOCIATIONS
*Happiness and contentment
in achieving success.*

REVERSE ASPECTS
Diminished forms of the above.

20
The Last Judgement

Since this card refers to the day of reckoning, its implications are of looking back, of taking stock of things that have happened. The dead are shown in the foreground of the card, rising from their graves, summoned by the blast on the trumpet of the angel who dominates the upper part of the card. The antithesis between the upright position and its reverse is clear-cut. In the first instance, there is cause for a satisfaction with a phase of life just completed; in the second, there may very well be remorse or regret.

KEY ASSOCIATIONS
Satisfactory outcome of a period of life or specific matter.

REVERSE ASPECTS
Regret over recent events; possible delay in concluding a sequence of actions.

21
The Universe

This card is one of the best demonstrations in the whole pack of just how rich Tarot symbolism is. A naked woman dances within the form of a laurel wreath, while the corners of the card harbour the Four Creatures of Ezekiel, which may evoke the four elements of matter and the four fixed signs of the Zodiac. A Christian reading of the Tarot could take them to represent Matthew, Mark, Luke and John. This is an especially positive card, indicating the successful completion of a phase of life and the promising start to the next.

KEY ASSOCIATIONS
Successful completion; a sense of repleteness.

REVERSE ASPECTS
Frustrations; inability to bring something to a satisfactory end.

Two types of card make up the four suits of the Minor Arcana: the Court cards which, unlike the conventional playing-card deck, include a Knight, and the Pip cards, so-called because only the suit symbols, or 'pips', were traditionally illustrated. The Aces, however, do stand somewhat apart since, in their singularity, they represent the very essence of their respective suits, each one of which is highly individual. For instance, Sceptres and Swords are

considered male suits, while Cups and Pentacles/Coins are
associated with the female principle. Fire is the element of
Sceptres, Water of Cups, Air of Swords, and Earth of
Pentacles/Coins. In general, too, the significance of the Minor
Arcana has much more to do with our everyday lives, in contrast
to the Major Arcana, which treat of the great underlying principles
of the universe.

KING of WANDS

The embodiment of responsibility and positive thinking, this King is often associated with the role of father. He is enterprising and caring in his upright position – considerate to others and fair in judgement. The strength of his personality, however, may only too easily turn to intolerance and, reversed, he can indicate an inability to appreciate other peoples' points of view, especially if he believes their moral standards are lower than his.

S.L. Macgregor Mathers, one of the most prominent occultists of the nineteenth century, associated this Queen with a woman living in the country, a lady of the manor. Like the King she is capable, but honest and fair in her dealings with other people. Indeed, the court cards are very much concerned with personal qualities and the Sceptres often express human action in achieving something rather than the significance of what is achieved. Reversed, the Queen's essential good nature may give way to a wish to dominate or even to bitterness.

THE QUEEN OF CLUBS

Sceptres knight

Of all the court cards, the Knights are very much an expression of movement and energy. In the case of the Knight of Sceptres, there is a suspicion that his actions, though well-meant, may remain uncompleted – a quality symbolized by the gap between the mouths and tails of the salamanders which decorate his doublet. There is, though, a negative side to the Knight, especially when reversed, in which his own enthusiasm and fiery quality are at odds with people around him, leading to discord and breakdown in relations.

Sometimes referred to as Pages, the Knaves represent the dominant quality of each suit in a more light-hearted way than their seniors in the pack. Thus, the positive and outgoing aspects of Sceptres take on the form of youthful enthusiasm, of the desire to bring light and excitement to people around. Of course, such an engaging set of characteristics can have its negative side. If circumstances are not propitious, then the Knave's simple, honest qualities can turn to petulance and weakness – a bearer of bad news.

VALET DE BÂTON

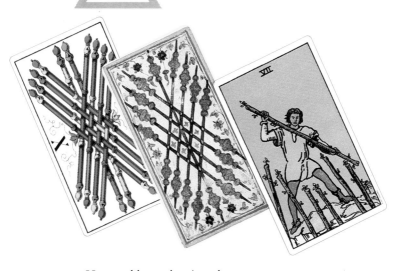

Sceptres
ten to six

TEN   Honourable conduct/treachery.
NINE   Discipline and order/disarray and delay.
EIGHT   Harmony and understanding/disagreement and dispute.
SEVEN   Successful advance/retreat and indecision.
SIX   Hopefulness/indecision.

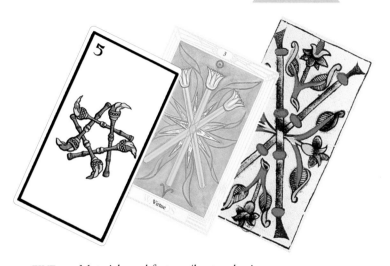

FIVE   Material good fortune / hurt and ruin.
FOUR   Four-square strength / unorthodox happiness and prosperity.
THREE   Commercial enterprise / reflection and stock-taking.
TWO   Success in material things / change, entering the unknown.

Sceptres
ace

The singularity of the aces implies a unique concentration of the major associations of the suit – in this case, Fire. Here is strength, power, creative inspiration and vast sexual energy, all expressed in the fecundity of the branch-like sceptre. This card is a veritable burst of energy and hope. But the sheer assertiveness of the card also means that the reverse is correspondingly catastrophic: chaos and ruin, perhaps because the great commitment and creativity of the Sceptres have been misdirected.

The Cups are associated with Water, a gentler, more soulful element than the Fire of the Sceptres. This is the force of the inner life and consequently, the King of Cups is a thinking person, perhaps a lawyer or doctor. That he is powerful is beyond doubt; we have only to note the way in which he grasps his cup, as though it were part of his regalia. Yet, he is quite a cool character and may be suspected of having a troubled inner life. Reversed, his undoubted creativity may involve him in dishonesty or corruption.

ROI DE COUPE

Cups
queen

This is an especially 'happy' card, indicating balance and harmony. The cup itself is always the most elaborate in the suit, as though to symbolize the high achievements made possible by the responsible use of the imagination. The Queen regards it almost lovingly, showing her concern that the forces symbolized should be directed towards worthy ends. Kindly, understanding, sometimes mysterious, she is undoubtedly an agent for good. Her spirituality, however, can appear as instability and fickleness, if the card is reversed.

Again, like the King and Queen, the Knight expresses the power of the creative forces of life, but he is less focused and less powerful than the two senior figures. Though well-meaning, he may sometimes give way to fantasy rather than use his imagination to get at the deeper truths of life. Indeed, there is often an ambivalence in his way of gazing at his cup, as though he is slightly uncertain of his true nature. His presence may herald change and new excitements, especially of a romantic nature but, reversed, there is unreliability and recklessness.

Prince of Cups

Cups
knave

The most innocent of the Cup court cards, the knave has yet to suffer the inner conflicts of his seniors. His gentle gaze falls uncomplicatedly upon his cup, shown in certain packs to contain a fish, symbol of imagination. Studiously confident, the Knave may represent undeveloped talents; his presence may indicate that a time for quiet reflection has arrived. The reverse position of this thoughtful young man is one of laziness, of neglect of skills, of failure to make meaningful commitments, of shallow self-indulgence.

Cups
ten to six

TEN   Good reputation and honour / strife and dispute.
NINE   Overcoming difficulty / falling into error.
EIGHT Security and attachment / fantasy and risk.
SEVEN Imaginative power / delusion and indecision.
SIX   Sense of the past / exaggerated nostalgia.

Cups
five to deuce

FIVE   Espousal and union /false starts.

FOUR   Apathy, dwelling on past experience /awakening to the new.

THREE   Wonder and joy /loss of happiness.

TWO   Affection, love /breakdown, ending.

An intense card, this Ace is the essence, the quiddity of love and all the positive powers of the unconscious mind. It bears, in various forms, the image of a great and elaborate cup, which can be identified with the Holy Grail, the repository of the Holy Ghost and the unifying force of the world. It was, however, the departure of the Grail from the land of King Arthur which brought about the downfall and disintegration of Camelot. Similarly, this card reversed is a symbol of disruption, of times changing for the worse.

KING OF SWORDS

The suit of Swords is most directly associated with the element of Air and therefore with matters of the spirit. But the sword is clearly a dangerous weapon and may cause pain and wounding but, by the same token, it can be used to cut through deception and subterfuge to arrive at a final truth. This King is a ruler indeed, a law-maker, a man of independent judgement, an achiever in whatever he does. The implications of a reversed card are alarming – probability of great disruption, abuse of power, contempt for the weak.

A courageous woman, the Queen may very well have suffered deep sorrow and loss. Somehow, however, with the aid of her sword, she has managed to overcome setbacks, achieving a sense of truth and inner wisdom. The sword is held erect, symbol of her moral rectitude; it also stands for the ability of women in general to come through suffering, especially at the hands of men, to a state of grace. We must beware, though, of the Queen reversed, of sorrow for sorrow's sake, of malice and wrongdoing in response to adverse circumstances.

Kali

Reine des Epées · Regina di Spade
Queen of Swords
Königin der Schwerter · Reina de Espadas

Swords
knight

KNIGHT of SWORDS .

Significantly, the Knight's sword is held at an angle or even brandished in the air. We may understand that although he is brave and skilful – he may even be a professional soldier – the Knight has a wild side to his character. This is greatly exaggerated when the card is reversed: bravery becomes impetuousness, skill at arms becomes the unnecessary use of force, application of great energy becomes simple-minded indulgence.

A card often associated with spying, of surveying the activity of other people, but from a detached point of view, the Knave raises himself above immediate conflict. Detachment is a very important quality for this figure, but if he does get more closely involved in any situation, then he will weigh up the pros and cons very carefully. There is, however, a side to the Knave which speaks of an inability to grasp the nettle, to act positively in adverse circumstances – the fatal flaw of Hamlet the Dane.

THE KNAVE OF SWORDS

Swords
ten to six

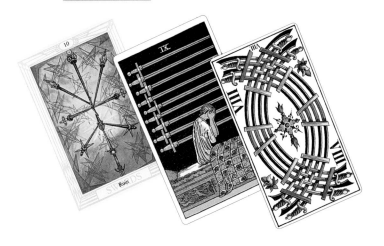

TEN   Misfortune and sorrow/temporary good fortune.

NINE   Tranquil conscience, good behaviour/suspicion and distrust.

EIGHT Oppression, illness/change, accident, liberation.

SEVEN Impulse, sudden desire/specific advice, counsel.

SIX   Gradual change, travelling/unexpected developments.

FIVE   Loss and defeat/accentuation of these.

FOUR   Withdrawal, retreat/return.

THREE Extreme pain and sorrow/mental and spiritual confusion.

TWO   Precarious balance in adversity, courage/violence and
             treachery.

Swords
ace

The Swords suit is very much a masculine one, associated with the ability to act rationally, but also with loss, pain and destruction. In its purest form, then, the Ace is the symbol of strongly constituted authority, of ability to pursue a line of enquiry to an ultimate truth. If this clarity is no longer there – when the card is reversed – then confusion and exaggeration in thought, feeling and deed will ensue.

The courtly figures of the Pentacles suit are much more down-to-earth than those of the rest of the Tarot pack. This underlines the nature of Pentacles as the magical sign for the world around us – a more actual presence than Air, Fire and Water. In some packs this is the suit of Coins, indicating an even more limited focus on the material world. Appropriately, then, the King looks more like a successful merchant than a regal figure. He is a capable man in his professional life, but still enjoys the comforts and delights of home and garden. His reversal implies failure and weakness.

THE KING OF MONEY

Pentacles
queen

QUEEN of PENTACLES

The Queen's closeness to the pulse of life is often evident in the intensity of the gaze she directs towards her pentacle. Sometimes this impression is reinforced by presenting her seated amid symbols of fecundity – a burgeoning garden, with roses and a rabbit. The patroness of Pentacles is the Empress, a passionate yet practical Trump card, and the Queen undoubtedly derives certain characteristics from this association – notably a generosity of soul, but tempered by a greater consciousness of the practical world. On the negative side, she may be pursued by self-doubt and distrust.

Pentacles
knight

A less adventurous fellow than the other Knights of the Tarot, the Knight of Pentacles displays an engaging simplicity and trustworthiness in his attitude to life. His existence may be rather uneventful, but he is dependable and will generally achieve his objectives in the fulness of time. Even the posture and bulk of his horse seem to suggest that this Knight has very little fantasy or romance in his life. This lack of adventure, of dash and bravura, becomes much more exaggerated if the card is reversed; what was practical commonsense becomes simply dullness.

Pentacles
knave

This youthful figure – possibly a student, but in any case someone setting out in life – is usually shown in close contemplation of his pentacle. It is as though he is completely caught up in his chosen discipline, to the exclusion of all outside matters. The dedication to his task and the seriousness which he brings to his work do make the Knave a very negative personage if the card is reversed. The careful, responsible approach is transformed into slow-wittedness and bumbling.

Pentacles
ten to six

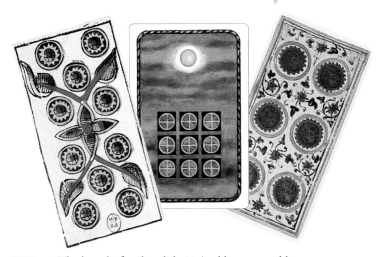

TEN   The hearth, family solidarity/recklessness and loss.

NINE   Patience, care/deception, unsound practice.

EIGHT   Attractiveness with modesty/superficiality, hypocrisy.

SEVEN   Venality, materialism/financial worry.

SIX   Offerings, satisfaction/unreasonable, overweening ambition.

Pentacles
five to two

FIVE   Partner, unspoilt love / lechery and licentiousness.

FOUR   Unalloyed pleasure / objection and prevention.

THREE High rank and public service / beginnings, unrewarding work.

TWO   Precarious balance, arranged pleasure / irresponsibility, forced jollity.

If the suit of Pentacles as a whole represents the varieties of well-being in the world around us, then the Ace is the quintessence of such feelings of contentment and happiness. Upright, the card has the positive connotations of enjoyment of everyday things, of a celebration of the bounty of nature, encapsulated especially in the form of the garden. Yet such wealth and plenty can also be seen as corrupting, as encouraging selfishness and over-indulgence in material comfort.

Sources of Illustrations

The following abbreviations have been used: *c* centre, *l* left, *r* right.

Naipes Heraclio Fournier S.A. 57*l*, 71*l*, 75, 78*l*; B.P. GRIMAUD 1981. With the kind authorization of FRANCE CARTES BP 49 - 54130 SAINT MAX - FRANCE 16, 28, 31, 39, 48, 53, 69, 73; Heron 18, 29, 33, 34, 40, 46*c*, 50, 51, 54, 57*r*, 60, 63*r*, 64*r*, 71*r*, 76, 77*l*; Aleister Crowley and Freida Harris, *Thoth Tarot Deck*, © 1970 Ordo Templi Orientis and AG Müller & Cie. Reproduced by permission and by courtesy of Samuel Weiser Inc., and U.S. Games Systems, Inc. 9, 15, 38, 46*l*, 57*c*, 61, 63*l*, 70*l*, 78*r*; © Photo Bibliothèque Nationale, Paris 14, 26, 36; Illustrations from tarot decks listed below and published by U.S. Games Systems, Inc., Stamford, CT 06902 USA, reproduced by permission. Further reproduction prohibited. Aquarian Tarot Deck, © 1970 U.S. Games Systems, Inc. 12, 42, 66. Barbara Walker Tarot Deck, © 1986 U.S. Games Systems, Inc. 67. Motherpeace Round Tarot Deck, © 1981, 1983 by Motherpeace, Inc. 32*l*. The Rider-Waite Tarot Deck ®, © 1971 by U.S. Games Systems, Inc. Copyright ©1993 Rider on behalf of the estate of A.E. Waite. All Rights Reserved 23, 37, 47, 52, 56*r*, 64*c*, 68, 70*c*, 74, 79. 1JJ Swiss Tarot Deck, © 1974 U.S. Games Systems, Inc. 3, 19, 24, 27, 32*r*, 44, 55, 56*l*, 59, 64*l*, 70*r*, 72, 78*c*. Pierpont Morgan-Bergamo Visconti-Sforza Tarocchi Deck © 1975, 1984 by U.S. Games Systems, Inc. 7, 12*r*, 35, 56*c*, 58, 63*c*, 77*r*. Charles Walker Collection & Images Colour Library Limited 5, 8, 10, 11, 17, 21, 22, 30, 41, 43, 45, 46*r*, 49, 62; Robert Wang 12*l*, 20, 25, 65, 71*c*, 77*c*.

British Library Cataloguing-in-Publication Data
A catalogue record for this book is available from the British Library

ISBN 0-500-06019-3

Printed and bound in Slovenia by Mladinska Knjiga